On That Happy Note

Dr. Sasi Taneja

India | USA | UK

Copyright © Dr. Sasi Taneja
All Rights Reserved.

This book has been self-published with all reasonable efforts taken to make the material error-free by the author. No part of this book shall be used, reproduced in any manner whatsoever without written permission from the author, except in the case of brief quotations embodied in critical articles and reviews.

The Author of this book is solely responsible and liable for its content including but not limited to the views, representations, descriptions, statements, information, opinions, and references ["Content"]. The Content of this book shall not constitute or be construed or deemed to reflect the opinion or expression of the Publisher or Editor. Neither the Publisher nor Editor endorse or approve the Content of this book or guarantee the reliability, accuracy, or completeness of the Content published herein and do not make any representations or warranties of any kind, express or implied, including but not limited to the implied warranties of merchantability, fitness for a particular purpose.

The Publisher and Editor shall not be liable whatsoever...

Made with ❤ on the BookLeaf Publishing Platform
www.bookleafpub.in
www.bookleafpub.com

Dedication

I dedicate this book to my parents

Honorable Mr. C Vijaya Kumar
Honorable Mrs. C S Lakshmi

They taught me to choose what is right, to stretch beyond my comfort and to keep going, while remaining true to who I am, through every waxing and waning moment of my life.

Preface

This collection is my humble attempt to share with you a few glimpses of life — the life of an ordinary girl who somehow stumbled into an extraordinary series of experiences (some welcome, some... let's just say "character-building").

These poems wander through a maze of emotions — from joy and nostalgia to confusion, heartbreak, and hope — occasionally tripping over themselves along the way, much like life itself.

I write of moments I've lived and witnessed: the quiet reverence for parents, the dizzy delight of falling in love, friendships that defy time zones, and the sheer relief of rain gracing Delhi's dusty summer heat. But life also has its darker shades — the ache of loss, the loneliness of distance, the heartbreak of broken promises, and the kind of disappointment that even chocolate can't fix.

Yet, running through it all, is one steady thread — **hope.**

Over time, I've realized there's always at least one way to solve any of life's problems. Sometimes it takes several wrong ways to find it — but that's part of the adventure.

And on rare occasions, the right answer is to stop trying entirely, brew yourself a cup of tea, and call it wisdom. If it brings peace to your mind, it usually *is*.

Life, after all, is a never-ending list of choices and actions. We choose how we act, and we choose how we react — though sometimes the latter happens before coffee. It took me years to learn the art of acting with happiness and hope (and I'm still a work in progress). You can do it too — should you choose to, and preferably before the next crisis arrives.

And so, on that cheerfully realistic note, I leave you with this collection.

It is my sincere hope that somewhere within these pages, you'll find a line, a thought, or a chuckle that feels a little like home.

Thank you for reading — and for letting my words borrow a few moments of your time.

Dr. Sasi Taneja

Acknowledgements

I would like to extend my heartfelt gratitude to every individual I've had the pleasure (and occasional bewilderment) of crossing paths with in life. From each one, I've learnt a lesson—some profound, others amusing—and together, they have all, in one way or another, contributed to the spirit and substance of this book. If I were to name everyone, I suspect the acknowledgments would outgrow the book itself (and possibly test your patience!).

A special note of thanks goes to my husband, **Siddhant**, my daughter, **Sarina**, and my son, **Savir** —my ever-reliable circle of energy, encouragement, and a delightful chaos that keeps the house (and my mind) from ever getting too quiet. You are the rhythm behind my songs and the joyful noise that keeps life endlessly entertaining.

Finally, my heartfelt appreciation to **Jade the Elemental** for the evocative cover art that so beautifully captures the soul of this collection. Your visual poetry brought my words to life in a way I could only have imagined.

1. An ode to my parents - Amma Nanna, this one's for you!

You planted my roots with love and care,
My branches reach for the sky you built.
My success a reflection of your rule and square,
With your blessing, all dreams fulfilled.

I sit, I crawl, I run, I fall,
You always hold my hand,
I laugh, I cry, sometimes wonder why...
You always help me understand.

I soar like an eagle flying around,
Your wisdom is the song I sing.
Although cliched as it may sound,
You ARE the wind beneath my wings.

Even when you had little, you gave me your best
Your golden dedication, your relentless gallantry,

You are golden doves, innocent and pure,
You are weavers of a fifty year tapestry.

With your love like a shield, I forge a new path,
Everything I am, you helped me to be,
My story written in the ink of your sacrifice,
Beneath my song, you are the quiet melody.

My existence bows in reverence every day,
You weathered many a storm together.
In my eyes, your dreams are alive,
I cherish your love, a legacy forever.

No words can express my gratitude enough,
I am forever indebted to you,
For you are the most humble, sincere and tough,
There is no me without you.

2. In the garden

On a partly cloudy, sunny day,
A little child who was all but two.
Scampered into the garden,
To find her favourite things to do.

There was magic in the trees,
Each petal and leaf, a friend anew,
Whispers in green blew in the breeze,
With every step the magic grew.

She spotted a blue butterfly on a red rose,
With wonder she watched them together,
The butterfly majestic, poised for a pose,
Dancing boldly in warm, golden weather.

She held up the butterfly just to say hello,
It looked at her with its big brown eyes,
Its wings fluttered, it wanted to go,
To fly against the deep blue skies.

So, she let the butterfly loose,
And watched it wave goodbye,
A yawn signaled her time to snooze,
Beneath the branches, with a soft sigh.

Now in her dreams, the garden stays,
Where the breeze and giggles often play,
With each new day, she'll return to her trees,
In the sun, the shade, forever free.

3. Rut of riot

This happened when we were six and four,
We stood in line for a can of milk.
Suddenly my father picked us up both,
To carry us home, swiftly.

The roads were lifeless gray lines,
The air was thick with unspoken dread,
I heard loud screams, saw a car on fire,
A man burnt inside until he was silent.

My father turned my face and covered my eyes,
I was whisked away, too scared to cry,
What followed had screams every night...
It was not for me to ask why.

A running man with a hunted animal's stare,
Behind him sickles of a frantic mob,
I couldn't move, I couldn't dare,
I wondered what we were living for?

The next few nights, the terror continued,
We whispered behind the blackened windows,
While we we clung to dreams of laughter,
We ventured to survive and be free.

Then dawn broke gently, whispered of hope,
The world outside, a tapestry of scars,
In the faces of strangers, I learnt to cope,
To weave my own story beneath the stars.

Often I dream I am in a labyrinth of fear,
Am I cursed to live with this fear every night?
But then I wake to the sound of laughter near,
The past may haunt, but I have learnt to fight.

4. The third Ashoka tree

The first Ashoka tree blossomed at this place.
In the sanctuary of bliss, an enchanted space,
A single heart, a single love, united as one,
No hiccups or hang-ups, just pure fun!

Come rain or shine, busy as bees,
And yet an ethereal calmness prevailed.
Empty pockets and meagre meals,
We sought small joys on life's trails.

The second Ashoka tree heralded a change,
A ghost in the library haunting the halls,
The shelter of a quiet harbor in range.
Building a bridge, the curtain falls.

We heard a chorus of different accents,
Voices of every land, skins of different hues,
Beneath our roof, the world converged,
There was a symphony of souls.

We broke bread with strangers,
Rhythmic drums of many nations,
Sailed to unseen lands without danger,
For it was time for new creations.

The third Ashoka tree carved the exit door,
To the life we knew as it was before,
We are rivers born of a single spring,
A stream that connects us, life will surely bring.

5. Mica, mica, everywhere

Oh child, my child, how quickly you turn nine,
Happy with rain or shine,
Blistering or bouncing, the roads resound,
With a laughter that's wholly divine.

Heat and the dust come twisting all around,
Howls and echoes come banging the doors,
Its welcome shadow drags in a respite,
What else could we ask for, what more?

The dust settles down as the rain pours galore,
My paper boats wade through the streams,
I wish wings would help me fly to the clouds,
Where shall l find the rainbow of my dreams?

When the sun returns to blaze,
The mica shines again, crystals and crystals everywhere,
The play goes on with unshaken hope,
For the twister shall surely come again.

6. Rose garden

Come let me tell you a well-worn story,
The favorite chapter from my book of life,
When I was twelve, I found a treasure,
A friend, a guardian, an angel alike.

We met at a game of basketball,
The game wasn't really her thing,
Our laughter still echoes in that court,
Our hearts connected by a string.

She was like the sun, and I the moon,
Different light, different paths we chose,
Yet, we were inseparable soon,
A perfect balance of day and night arose.

I was the free-spirited sail,
On a new quest every day.
She was my grounding anchor,
Who kept us from drifting away.

Her laughter danced like leaves in a breeze,
We shared secrets by the rose garden behind,
Oft I went to this sanctuary of peace,
Moments of joy, just one of a kind.

Time marched on and our homes moved far,
The string holding us stretched but never broke,
Each memory a brushstroke on the canvas of my heart,
In the gallery of life, her laughter still spoke.

Through storms when my sailboat rocked,
She was always my guiding light.
In the rhythm of life, our own sweet refrain,
Though paths may diverge, we still belong,
In the silent echoes, love will remain.

7. Shadows in a wrestle

Loneliness is a curse, also a boon,
If only I had listened, if only I had known.
For this time is here, for better or for worse,
I love being alone, and I loathe being alone.

Did I fall behind? Or did I feel behind?
Love and Lone are two sides of a coin,
Am I a good brother? Are you a good sister?
With victory on one side and nought the other.

The music in my ears says don't turn around,
The light in my face shows me the way,
Alone I toil into the still of the night,
Wrestling shadows that refused to sway.

Come home, my brother, for your sister awaits,
Do we really have to pay this cost?
Am I that sister from your cherished childhood,
The childhood that never was truly lost.

Yet time is a river, swift and unkind,
Flowing through memories of laughter and tears,
Can we mend the bridge that distance has wrought,
Or is our bond caught in the web of our fears?

8. Sunset at Andrews Court

The dewdrops hang and the chapel bell rings,
The winter fog crawls across the ground,
When my hands are cold and the birds all sing,
That's when you and I are found.

Our paths crossed, or were they never apart?
A tender strength that holds us in a bind
It takes a rock garden that we have forgotten
It takes a force that's one of a kind.

When we lose our way and yet we stay,
laughing in the cool summer breeze,
When you watch my eyes against the blue skies,
Play that song for me, could you please?

For this desert rose the rain is sunshine
In Andrews court together we watch the sun set.
When I think of you on a Saturday night,
When I love you but not just yet.

9. Hot ziti in a cold town

From far far away to live happily ever after,
This fairy tale holds all in between,
Laughter and pain, all over again,
This did happen, whether heard or seen.

My journey across the seven seas,
Seven streams for me to find,
Seven times I fell and pulled me up
Seven dreams I left behind.

Now it wasn't always all bad,
Some days were happy too,
I caught fresh snowflakes with thrill,
I walked the nights under the moon.

Around the corner was a wonderful man,
I wonder how it happened to be…
Was it a chance or a choice, one may never know,
Was it a gift just right for me?

My journey across the seven seas,
Seven streams for me to find,
Seven times I fell and pulled me up
Seven dreams I left behind.

I was by the lake near a big bald tree,
The platform there just chilled my bones,
The phone booth there sung the right songs for me,
Someday, Yellow taxi and Mr. Jones.

The man on the heat vent asked me to give,
And I did everything I could,
For I am neither selfish, nor manipulative,
Hot baked ziti did him real good.

My journey across the seven seas,
Seven streams for me to find,
Seven times I fell and pulled me up
Seven dreams I left behind.

A knight in shining armour awoke
Riding high on a moonlit night,
Awaiting, hopeful and lucky savant,
Knotted to a future so bright.

So here i went, alone again,
Seven more streams to find,

To a future that eagerly awaited me
Seven more dreams in mind.

10. Destiny of promise or promise of destiny?

When I say I will, I will, I will.
When you say I will, you will if it suits you.
The destiny of promise is to reach its end,
Then why, oh why do you not see it through?

Patience and longing don't see eye to eye,
Like a seesaw of joy and pain,
One foot in hope and one stuck in hell,
I root for hope time and again!

Blessed I am to have those who love me,
Blessed I am to have those who hurt me,
Many a dream rushed, many a times crushed,
Is it then in fact a promise of destiny?

Yet in the darkness, a flame remains,
A whisper of futures not yet defined,
With scars as my earth, I walk through the rains,
And gather the pieces of what's intertwined.

Each moment a pearl in a string that's a boon,
Strung by hands both tender and strong,
In heartbeats of fervor, I fly toward the moon,
With questions that linger, but dreams that belong.

11. Midnight star

Come alive together, hand in hand we wander,
In the garden of hope where memories sprout,
With petals of joy, our love grows fonder,
Warmth of our stories comes about.

For I am a moon, in the depths of the night,
My beloved star at midnight found,
In the hush of night, our laughter takes flight,
Our dreams cherished with love and trust,

The star and moon together begun,
Around the clouds, frolic and fun.
Maps all backwards, our world upside down,
Yet in unison, we behold the same crown.

Love and loss, two sides of a coin,
Desolate devotion combine,
In whispers of moonlight, hearts intertwine,
Through shadows of heartache, our spirits align.

No death can part us, such is our bind,
For we shall be together again,
Another life, another turn, each one of a kind,
Our dreams will forever remain.

Hand in hand, we'll traverse an endless expanse,
Each heartbeat a promise, a vibrant romance,
In the dance of the cosmos, our souls will ignite,
Together we'll shine, two beacons of light.
With each twinkle above, our love's lullaby,
Echoes through ages, a sweet, timeless sigh.

12. Toddler playgroup

Cackle of children in the park,
Screeching swings, sand, and sunshine,
Sight and sounds of a day divine.

Little tots play until dark,
Running in circles around the slide,
They are teachers' pets and mothers' pride.

Laughter dances on the breeze,
Giggling whispers weave through trees,
Fragrant flowers waltzing with the bees.

Tiny hands grasp at their tools,
Chasing shadows, unafraid to glide,
In this world, their dreams collide.

In twilight's glow, their magic twirls,
Mirthful moments in a dance unfurls,
Forever cherished in heart of pearls.

13. Night bird in a café

I waited for my night bird, in a cafe', I dare say,
Although I saw a straight game, they played their own play.

They came to me as a gift, a beautiful angel of light
A foal that gazed through blue-grey eyes, shining ever so bright.

O untamed one, I love you so,
forever this way you be
I'd give the whole wild west to you,
If it were up to me.

They made known, quite early on, they got their own mind
No mould could fit no matter, they're their own kind

Different and unafraid, the strongest ever seen
A soaring eagle with a clear head, the sharpest ever been.

O untamed one, I love you so,
forever this way you be
I'd give the whole sky to you,
If it were up to me.

Drivers of their own life, when they know, they know for sure
Dazzling clarity is a given, this jade is a gem so pure.

O untamed one, I love you so,
forever this way you be
I'd give all the jewels to you,
If it were up to me.

Nothing can ever stop them, nothing they cannot play.
When they decide to go, nothing can stand in their way.

I believe in my night bird, they sing the perfect song,
No tempest can break, no daydream can take, they'll choose where they belong.

O untamed one, I love you so,
forever this way you be
I'd give the whole world to you,
If it were up to me.

The sun's setting in the window, the orange sky aglow,
The beautiful birdsong stays with me no matter where I go.

14. Red bricks and tile tricks

As I entered the firm and fostering gates,
Deep within was a newfound peace,
The very ground beneath felt hallowed,
Coconut trees, like angels, heralding in the breeze.

Like a pilgrim reaching limitless bliss,
I walked in with reverence and a smile.
The story of tradition and endurance,
Was evident in the brick and tile.

I asked a young lady, is there a vacancy?
Yes, please do fill the form, said she graciously,
I asked my little one is this where you'd like to be?
Her eyes wide with wonder, her sound pure discovery.

My child's giggles by the laughing fountain,
Was a whisper of tomorrow's promise,
In that sound I heard the future,
The waters of pure, enduring bliss.

Although the path ahead was veiled,
An undeniable calling, a chorus of many reasons,
Led me to join this incredible journey,
A journey that would span eighteen seasons.

My young saplings joined this seedbed
In the fertile soil of the classroom,
There the gentle gardeners tended,
With love for the students to bloom.

With patience and care, they nurtured the minds,
Their love like glowing embers, deep and warm,
They weaved their dreams, helped them find,
Through the twists and turns, each lesson a charm.

Like a mango that ripens and falls,
I give thanks to the tree where they grew.
Beneath its branches, memories call,
In shadows of grace, their spirits anew.

Together we've journeyed, in darkness and bright,
With each step forward, we carry their light,
A legacy forged in each laugh and each tear,
In the tapestry of time, forever linked here.

As our journey nears its final horizon,
As the twilight deepens on our long road,

My mind cherishes every moment,
My heart overflows with gratitude.

Our children will keep the flame burning
Our future is tied to theirs,
No rain or hail, can stop a sun from turning,
Their radiant spirits, a force that declares.

In every challenge, they'll rise and learn,
With roots enriched by the love they received,
They'll carry our hopes, with passion they'll yearn,
For a world where kindness and courage are believed.

So here I stand, not in sorrow but in pride,
A proud witness to the tapestry we've spun,
Through laughter and lessons, side by side,
In the promise of tomorrow, our hearts beat as one.

15. Mary's dream

Behold, a leader is born.

Born into a world of thorns,
A stalwart, he remained undeterred,
With love, power and mercy,
A soulful king, a guide, a shepherd.

Hurt lost many a time, he's no stranger to pain,
Yet his heart remained sincerely true,
He's shielded by courage unwavering,
He dares to dream of skies so blue.

My angel of joy, with him I win,
The dreams I dream for him.
For he weaved a new fashion of thought,
He strode with purpose, with passion he fought.

He smiles with fortitude and stoic sufferance,
His calm resolve feeds his endurance.
He commands the music, he blazes a trail,

A resilient victor, he shall prevail.

In shadows he walks, yet seeks out the light,
A beacon of hope in the darkest of night,
With wisdom in whispers, he forges a new way,
Inspiring the weary, igniting their sway.

With laughter like sunshine, and kindness as gold,
He nurtures the young, the young and old,
Each step he takes leaves footprints of grace,
In a world where compassion finds its rightful place.

When you're in need, he's the friend indeed,
He reads you better than you do.
He tells you just what you need,
You're dauntless, when he's with you.

So listen up, it's time to pay heed,
Forever we'll flourish, together we'll need,
A leader like him, with a heart so true,
Who'll carve out a future, bright, just for you.

With embers of courage, he'll fan the small spark,
Turning visions to life, igniting the dark,
He's the fire we cherish, the flame that won't cease,
A melody woven with threads of our peace.

Behold, he is here.

16. So soon monsoon

It seemed life was in slow motion,
Last summer, scathed parched to no end,
But life pressed on with utmost devotion,
   With hope of rain around the bend.

Then came one splendid blushing eve,
A squall banged many a door,
Far on the west horizon it was,
A grey pelter like never before.

With each droplet's childlike hug
The parched soil smiled in glee,
Life awakened to an endless rapture,
The koel bird sang merrily.

The sun was missing for days,
The air was cold every night,
A symphony of scents of monsoon lingered,
As nature danced in delight.

Joyful I danced in the rain, behold,
My dreams mingled with rain-soaked grass
My world felt alive, colorful and bold,
In sudden dismay I watched the clouds pass.

Now, after the clouds bid adieu
There still remained a dream or two,
With hope and hubris, I called the clouds back,
Too proud to heed, they'll return when they do.

17. Hello! God, is that you?

A teacher of dreams, a beacon of hope
A garden of comfort, a healing shade,
Ma, you are the patient angel,
A quiet guardian of my soul

You bestow glory on me,
With gentle words that softly unfold,
You paint my path with colors bright,
And wrap my fears in stories told.

You teach me strength in every fall,
To rise again, to stand up tall,
In every word, your love's a call,
A melody that sings through all.

In every lesson, you've sown the seeds,
Of strength and courage, bold and true,
With every hug, you know my needs,
A lighthouse, guiding me anew.

Through seasons changing, you've stayed by me,
A compass when I've lost my way,
Your wisdom flows like a timeless sea,
A constant tide, come what may.

So here's my heart, laid bare and true,
For all the dreams you've helped me chase,
In gratitude, I honor you,
My guiding star, my sacred space.

18. A stitch in time

Love blossomed with a canopy of care,
There was peace, bliss, calm sublime,
With roots that stretch deep, dreams shared,
They were a vine entwined in time.

When he spoke the language her spirit knew,
Her soul exhaled, for it was seen,
When they didn't just hear the words,
They listened to the silence in between.

Once solid walls began to crumble,
A fractured fortress beneath a cloud,
With hollow laughter, they were torn asunder,
They were together alone in doubt.

Amidst this storm lay a house divided
A casualty of war let out a silent scream
Her memories bandaged in shadow of guilt,
An emotional orphan clutching a dream.

She wears a crown of thorns of others' mistakes,
She sees only the splinter in your eye
The guilt isn't hers to take,
It's not her fault when vases fly.

And when the storm abates, as sun softly sighs,
Embrace all the fragments; let courage arise.
For through every storm, love's light will remain,
A beacon of hope, erasing the pain.

So gather the pieces, let them be whole,
With each gentle stitch, mend the deep soul.
In the warmth of connection, find solace anew,
Where shadows once lingered, let sunbeams break through.

In the echoes of laughter, the silence will heal,
Casting away doubts, the truth they conceal.
Let love be the lantern, guiding your way,
For hearts that are tender will always stay.

19. Safety car and pitstops

Once as a child,
With flayed knees and a festive heart,
Carefree and oblivious to my parents' part.
My parents the crucible,
Forging my life from laughter's spark,
Absorbing all misery from the dark.
Fast forward to this time,
Now I am a parent the crucible,
Forging my children's life from laughter's flame,
Following wisdom as my safety car,
Shielding them from shadows scar.
For I am a relentless driver
I may choose to pitstop, a phase,
But I will not quit the race.

Through winding roads and life's strains,
I teach them to dance in the relentless rains.
With every laugh and tear they've shed,
I map a future, where dreams are bred.
I chase many a sunrise, bright and wide,

With passions ignited, they'll take the ride.
Hand in hand, we'll face the dawn,
For in their smiles, my worries are gone.
And though the tires may wear with time,
In this journey together, we will climb.

My parents in their golden years,
And I am in my prime,
We move forward with pride,
Holding onto love that never veers.
Safety cars and pitstops, tune-up for our team
Winds of change that raise us closer to our dreams.
Like branches of a tree reaching for the sun,
In this crucible of life, we are one.
With every challenge, we rise and shine,
In our eyes, the past and future intertwine.

20. Java good

A fragrant cloud of coffee and caramel,
Soft yellow lights to set the mood,
Music and murmur make a symphony of delight,
At this small coffee shop called Java good.

An oasis of peace, a haven of mirth,
In the warm embrace of soft, velvet air,
We welcome ideas, new connections take birth,
In this sanctuary, love and laughter we share,

There once came a man with a perky smile,
Chatting me up about his day,
His laughter danced like the steam from my cup,
As stories unfolded in a warm ballet.

As time passed slowly, there was the soft ring,
As the orders kept rolling in,
But here at Java mode, we linger,
With the sweetness of friendship within.

A book beckoned me from the corner shelf,
Filled with stories of a world so far,
Its pages whispered secrets to my heart,
Promising adventures beneath the stars.

I curled up in the nook, the scent of brewed dreams,
Losing myself in every line, each tale,
Where dragons soared by the prancing streams,
In this cozy retreat, love did not fail.

The man returned, his smile still bright,
"Got lost in a story, did you?" he teased,
And as he settled in, our laughter took flight,
In this little corner, our hearts were pleased.

With every sip, the moments stretched,
Time paused to listen, suspended in glee,
Amongst the rich blend of coffee and dreams,
At Java good, it was just you and me.

21. There's always a way...

When you're not sure which way to go,
When you're just too afraid to say no,
When things aren't going quite as planned,
When you think you're falling, awaiting land.

You may have came at the wrong time,
You may be stuck in the wrong game,
When everything looks upside down.
Or you may be feeling shame.

You must ask yourself, is this really me?
Is there something I can do differently?
Only when its darker, you'll see a lamp dimly lit,
There's always a way to go, you just have to find it.

What's wrong? You wonder endlessly...
Is it them, or is something wrong with me?
You search for clues in the silence of night,
Keep asking the questions, keep holding on tight.

What worked before, works no more,
You start losing the faith in you,
Each step seems heavier, each choice a weight,
The mirror reflects a stranger, tempting fate.

You must ask yourself, is this really me?
Is there something I can do differently?
Only when its darker, you'll see a lamp dimly lit,
There is always a way to go, you just have to find it.

You must trust this journey, let the path unfold,
In the depths of your struggle, you are bold.
So wade through the darkness, as your heart sings,
For even in chaos, you will find your wings.

Epilogue

This began as a dare and somehow turned into a map—a journey through the terrain of my own emotions, where I stumbled upon old feelings and traced each fragile fault line hidden in the gaps. I've already come a long way, though there is still so much more to do. I remain deeply grateful every single day for those who gently guided me along the way.

To my family, my first and constant light, you taught my heart how to stay steady and true. And to those who are at the edge of uncertainty, facing their own dark nights, remember this: hold on to hope — there is always a way, and you will find it.

www.ingramcontent.com/pod-product-compliance
Lightning Source LLC
Chambersburg PA
CBHW070500050426
42449CB00012B/3062